MALALA YOUSAFZAI

WARRIOR WITH WORDS

By Karen Leggett Abouraya

Illustrated by L.C. Wheatley

StarWalk KidsMedia

Dedicated to my mother, Jean Leggett, for her unshakable dedication to education, for herself, her children, and her students. —K. L. A.

For J.B. & N.P. —L. C. W.

AP Photo/Jessica Rinaldi, File

Published by StarWalk Kids Media
Contact: Starwalk Kids Media, 15 Cutter Mill Road, Suite 242, Great Neck, NY 11021

www.StarWalkKids.com

ISBN 978-1-63083-316-9 (paperback)

StarWalk KidsMedia

Malala is a miracle in pink. Malala is a warrior with words. Malala Yousafzai did not celebrate her sixteenth birthday with a sleepover, but with a stand-up.

It was a miracle that she could stand at all. She stood up in front of the whole world to prove that words have power.

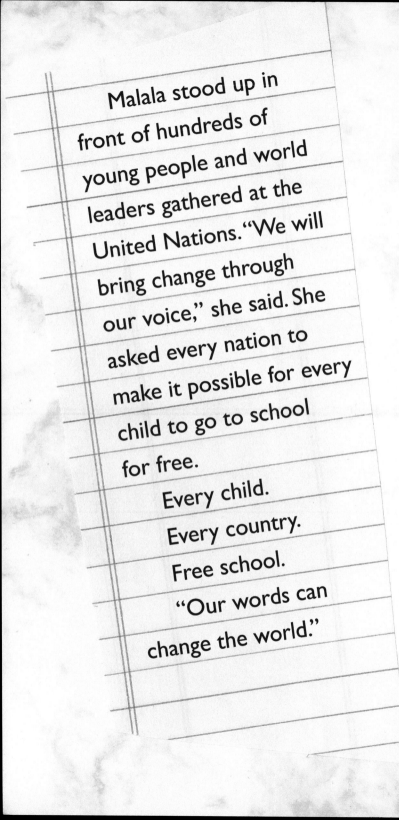

Malala stood up in front of hundreds of young people and world leaders gathered at the United Nations. "We will bring change through our voice," she said. She asked every nation to make it possible for every child to go to school for free.

Every child.
Every country.
Free school.
"Our words can change the world."

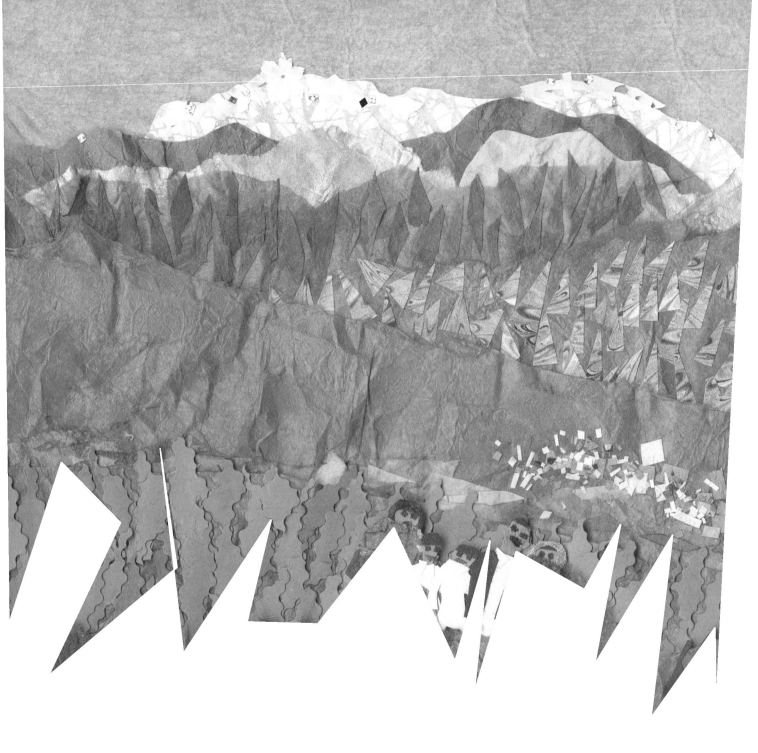

Where did Malala learn what she could do with her voice and her words?

Malala was born in Mingora on the River Swat in northern Pakistan. She remembers "my Swat" as a land of sweet green valleys and mountains shimmering with snow where people came to refresh their spirits and be together with their families.

Malala's mother was the heart of their home. She is quiet, but she is a strong and determined supporter of her daughter. Malala's two little brothers kept chickens. Malala kept books and also a notebook filled with her own words. Malala's father named his daughter after Malala of Maiwand, a brave woman whose poetry helped save her village from invaders more than 100 years ago.

When the Taliban came to power in the Swat Valley, they said girls should not go to school. Malala's father, Ziauddin Yousafzai, was the principal of a school for girls. He encouraged his daughter to tell the world about those difficult days. Malala wrote a blog that was printed in her native Urdu and also in English by the British Broadcasting Corporation (the BBC). She used the name Gul Makai so that no one would know who was really writing the blog.

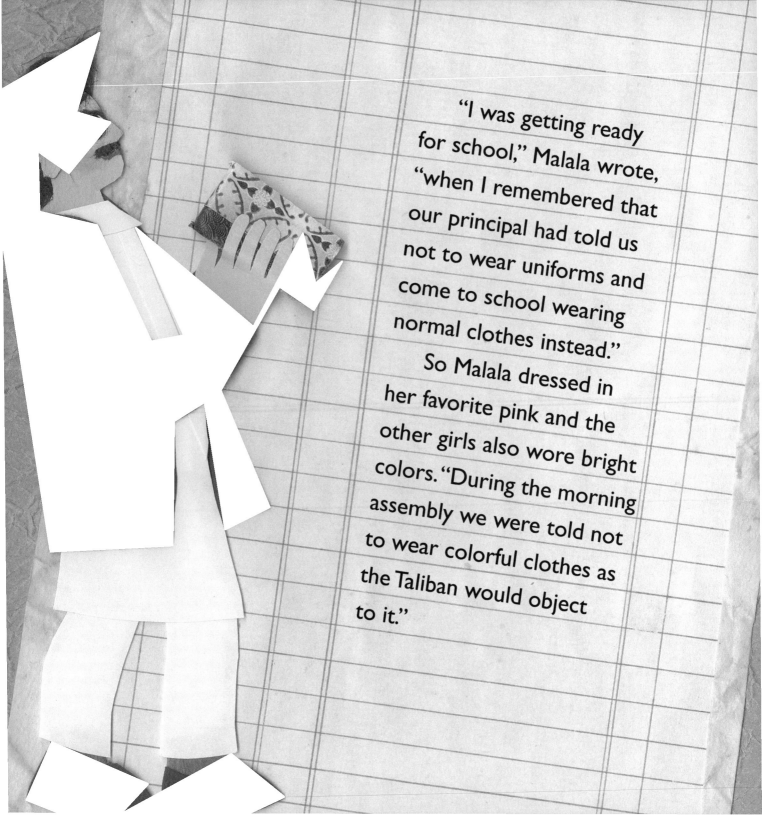

"I was getting ready for school," Malala wrote, "when I remembered that our principal had told us not to wear uniforms and come to school wearing normal clothes instead." So Malala dressed in her favorite pink and the other girls also wore bright colors. "During the morning assembly we were told not to wear colorful clothes as the Taliban would object to it."

The Taliban ordered everyone to obey very strict rules. They said that girls should not be educated and women should not work outside their homes. Malala wrote that this was a very dark time.

"We have some people who are afraid of ghosts and some people who are afraid of spiders, and in Swat we were afraid of humans like us."

Just before winter vacation, the Taliban announced that all schools for girls in the Swat Valley would close on January 15. Many of Malala's friends were afraid. Only 11 students came to a class that normally had 27 children.

That spring, when Pakistan's army began fighting the Taliban, Malala and her family left the Swat Valley. "Leaving home was like we would be apart from our heart," Malala wrote, "because our home was our heart. I had to leave my books and my bag and my school."

When the fighting was over, Malala's family returned to Mingora. The destruction made them weep. The house was in chaos. Her brothers' chickens had died. But, miraculously, the books in her room had not been touched. "They are very precious," she wrote.

Her father's school opened again,
but many other schools had been destroyed.

"Education is our basic right!"

Malala was sad and angry. She began writing and speaking out to everyone who would listen and she did not hide her name anymore. Malala wanted to prove that peaceful words have power over violence.

Every day she went to school with her pink backpack and filled the pages of her notebook with words. "Education is our basic right," she wrote. She won Pakistan's first National Youth Award for Peace in 2011.

On October 9, 2012, when she was riding home from school, a man from the Taliban climbed on the bus and shot Malala and two of her friends. Her friends were able to recover in Pakistan, but Malala had been shot on the side of her head. She was taken to a hospital in England that specializes in treating wounded soldiers. Her family and friends feared she might not live.

Miraculously, Malala recovered with no injury to her brain.

She spoke at the United Nations only nine months after the shooting.

"Nothing changed in my life except this," Malala declared, "weakness, fear, and hopelessness died. Strength, power, and courage were born. I am the same Malala. My ambitions are the same. My hopes are the same. My dreams are the same."

Malala and her brothers are now going to school in England. Malala is sharing her dreams and her words around the world. People around the world are answering with rallies, prayer vigils, and marches, singing, "I am Malala."

With support from her parents and many other people, she started the Malala Fund to give girls hope for a better life. Forty girls in Malala's beloved Swat are now in school because of the Malala Fund. Malala talks to them regularly on Skype. Other girls are sharing their stories on the Malala Fund website.

Malala says her dream is to be a politician and help save her country. In 2013, the European Parliament awarded Malala the Sakharov Prize for Freedom of Thought, because of her courage in defending the right of all children to be educated.

Malala is a miracle in pink. She is a warrior with words. She wants every boy and girl to stand up and speak out for the millions of children who are not able to go to school all over the world.

"Let us pick up our books and pens. One child, one teacher, one pen and one book can change the world."

Pakistan:
Important Dates in the Life of a Nation

Malala Yousafzai and her family are Pashtun, a proud people who belong to about 60 different tribes. The Pashtun people are Muslims who live in Afghanistan and Pakistan.

The territories that are now Afghanistan, Pakistan, and India were once part of the British Empire. The British Parliament voted to end British control over India in 1947. Muhammad Ali Jinnah united Muslims in India and worked hard to create an independent homeland for his people. In 1947, the Islamic Republic of Pakistan was established as a majority Muslim country and India became a majority Hindu country.

At first, Pakistan had two parts with India in the middle. There have been several wars between India and Pakistan, usually because of disagreements about their borders. In 1971, East Pakistan became the independent country of Bangladesh.

Benazir Bhutto

In 1988, Benazir Bhutto became Prime Minister of Pakistan, the first female prime minister in an Islamic country. Malala greatly admires Benazir Bhutto and considers her a role model. Benazir Bhutto was assassinated in Pakistan in 2007.

Rise of the Taliban

"Talib" is the word for "student" in Pashto and Arabic. The Taliban are Pashtuns who come from religious schools that teach a very strict, conservative form of Islam. Along with other groups, they fought to end control of Afghanistan by the former Soviet Union (now Russia) from 1979 to 1996, when the Taliban took power in Afghanistan. They also wanted to control parts of Pakistan where Pashtun Muslims lived, especially the northwestern areas like the Swat Valley.

In July 2009 the Pakistani Army announced that it had defeated the Taliban in Swat. Families returned to Mingora and the Swat Valley. However, the Taliban remain in Swat and many other areas of Pakistan and Afghanistan even today, seeking to return to power.

Resources on Pakistan

BBC Pakistan profile:
www.bbc.co.uk/news/world-south-asia-12965779

Baltimore County, MD, Public Schools—Pakistani Heritage Resource Packet:
http://bcps.org/offices/oea/pdf/cultural_heritage/Pakistani-Heritage-Resource-Packet.pdf

What's it like to live in Pakistan?
www.timeforkids.com/destination/pakistan/day-in-life

You Can Help

Do you remember being excited the first time you had your own backpack or climbed on a school bus? Too many children in the world never know that excitement. Those are the children Malala wants to help.

- 57 million children around the world are not going to school. That's the same as all the people who live in California and New York combined.

- As many as half the children in countries where there is war or violence are not able to go to school.

- Almost two-thirds of Pakistan's poor girls have never been to school at all.

Many organizations are working to help boys and girls get to school.

The Malala Fund was started by Malala and her friends and family. The executive director of the Fund is Shiza Shahid, another young Pakistani woman who graduated from Stanford University in the United States and once organized a summer camp for Malala and other girls in the Swat Valley. Shiza says, "Teaching someone you know who isn't going to school or helping someone who is suffering or focusing your career on what you believe will make a difference in the future. We all have ways to make a difference."

School Girls Unite was started in Maryland by middle school girls who talked with young women from Mali about the unfair treatment of girls in many poor countries. Together these girls created an action guide called "Girls Gone Activist." They also lobbied to start an International **Day of the Girl**, which is now celebrated every year on October 11.

The United Nations Foundation's **Girl Up** gives American girls the chance to become world leaders, beginning by creating their own girls clubs.

Girl Rising is a film about nine extraordinary girls in Cambodia, Haiti, Nepal, Egypt, Ethiopia, India, Peru, Sierra Leone, and Afghanistan—each one battling many obstacles to go to school.

Global Campaign for Education works to improve education for both boys and girls, all over the world.

Although many of these organizations are especially working with girls, Malala is speaking up for girls *and* boys who are not able to go to school. "Dear brothers and sisters, we want schools and education for every child's bright future," said Malala at the United Nations.

For more information on these organizations and how you can help, look up their websites on the Internet.

StarWalk Kids Library

Read, Grow, Excel

If you liked this book, you'll LOVE these:

CPSIA information can be obtained at www.ICGtesting.com
Printed in the USA
BVIW12n2046210516
448551BV00009B/96